NOW

The Ohio Arts Council helped fund this organization with state tax dollars to encourage economic growth, educational excellence and cultural enrichment for all Ohioans.

The Miami University Press Poetry Series
General Editor: James Reiss

NOW

*For Don
with
admiration*

[signature]

A collection of poems
by

~~Judith Baumel~~

[signature]

Miami University Press

Oxford, Ohio

Library of Congress Cataloging-in-Publication Data

Baumel, Judith, 1956 -
   Now : a collection of poem/by Judith Baumel.
      p. cm. – (The Miami University Press poetry series)
      ISBN 1-881163-14-8. – ISBN 1-881163-15-6
   I. Title. II Series.
PS3552.A845N69 1996   95-34502
811'.54 – dc20   CIP

The paper in this book meets the guidelines
for permanence and durability of the Committee
on Production Guidelines for Book Longevity
of the Council on Library Resources. ∞

Printed in the U.S.A.

9 8 7 6 5 4 3 2 1

For Sam and Aaron

ACKNOWLEDGMENTS

I would like to thank the following periodicals and anthologies in which a number of these poems first appeared—at times in different versions:

The Agni Review: "The Park Of The Monsters," "Philips Street, Andover"

The Denver Quarterly: "Einstein's Curse"

Harvard Magazine: "From The Town Of Castle Ruins On The Skirts Of The Mountain Range"

Indiana Review: "Malleus Maleficarum"

The New Criterion: "And Boaz Begat Obed, And Obed Begat Jesse, And Jesse Begat David," "Vandalism"

The New Yorker: "World Without End," "You Weren't Crazy And You Weren't Dead," "Jupiter Evening Star"

The New Republic: "Custard Of The Pawpaw"

Pivot: "New, New York"

The Tennessee Quarterly: "Patinage Au Polygone — Grenoble 1900"

The Threepenny Review: "Thumbs Up"

Articulations: The Body And Illness In Poetry (University of Iowa Press): "Let Me In"

Under 35: The New Generation of American Poets (Anchor / Doubleday): "Fish Speaking Veneto Dialect"

My thanks to the Corporation of Yaddo in whose peaceful precincts some of these poems were written.

"it still seemed that some other time,
from some other place, had invaded the town
and was silently establishing itself."

—Aharon Appelfeld

CONTENTS

Now

THUMBS UP

On certain fall mornings it's possible to walk Eighteenth
from Tenth to First into a white sun blinding the tunnelled street.
From within that obliterating light come shades,
figures loading and unloading cargo, holding briefcases or babies,
leaning on fire trucks. The hints of two seasons cross in the air,
as, on either end of the extreme school year,
shuffling curious September or restless June,
the humid New York heat will descend on classrooms
where even under high ceilings the thick air becomes torture.
Onto the old half-varnished seats little legs pour moisture
through the clean wool plaid of new school clothes, thinking
New Year's, thinking Columbus Day, thinking Thanksgiving,
or through cotton sundresses, waiting for hydrants and hoses
        and pools,
and the teacher despairing, shuts the lights for an illusion
        of coolness.
In the gift of half dark children rest their heads on desks,
        some brood,
some notice the vegetable smell of soft old wood.
They all begin Thumbs Up: Heads down, fists closed, thumbs
up, one child wanders the room to touch a random waiting thumb
whose owner may go down the hall to the water fountain,
return, and touch another, and so through slow and slower time
all thumbs, all mouths are touched, each knowing
the approach of the next, subtly, through that dark flow,
each growing up into the shuffle of new mornings gnarled
with purpose, out on the streets, watching the world's
business emerge from the shadows, come into relief, stop caught,
go past, and be finally as brilliant, seen backward, as Plato taught.

NEW, NEW YORK

I love the way this city remakes
itself over and over, throwing memory
to the wind of the glass and steel
canyons, an organism of noise
replicating itself higher and higher,
one makeshift elevator after another.

And I love the unremarkable history
scattered in glass pavement tiles,
light let into underground cafes
where Melville and Whitman drank,
now sitting beneath scaffolding, beneath
the Italianate facades of development.

Nothing like Rome-The-Eternal,
that hands-on-museum of civilization,
nor like Sepino where the Roman theater
gave up gracefully to medieval houses,
a spontaneous architecture on the stones
of conquerors. Children of Samnites,
children of goats of Samnites, together
in big beds in dark rooms that skipped
a Renaissance of humanity and light.

We walked there when everything was new
for us, your hands smoothing la porta
Benevento, your eyes reviving the water
mill, the oil vats, the thermal baths.

Wandering the silent reticulated walls,
you were dark in Molise, back-town Italy,
while here you translate to me the throb
of machinery, the electricity of the sidewalk
generators dotting the streets that feed you,
here where newness is our very first name
and our last, the latest invention of repetition.

You Weren't Crazy and You Weren't Dead

Four neat sonnets ago we were twenty.
You weren't crazy and you weren't dead.
We still counted ourselves four girlfriends
who'd gone to Radcliffe from the Bronx.

Later, nervous elegies, those four boxy
sonnets, emerged from my stunned hand.
I didn't have the courage to write them to you,
but to your parents, survivors again.

Your name in the synagogue's blue glass window
panel always makes me cry, and in the film
over my eyes I collect square Polaroids
of Purim costumes, graduations, day camps,

the mean permutations of the cubic friendship:
who was whose best friend, who telling secrets
to whom, who prettiest, smartest, the showoff, the bore.
A story of small, sorry memories.

The year after you killed yourself
the rest of us took a four-bedroom apartment.
The fourth was always changing owners.
We mentioned your name from time to time.

Your brother named his baby girl after you.
He seemed to leave the names of those others lost
in the war in the war.
I try to find comfort in this birth, this life,

the odd fact of another child with this name.
And, astonished that we have grown up, become mothers
five times over among the three of us,
the old numbers jumbled somehow and you

somehow gone out, away, or stayed behind,
I find the image of another, still young
Emily toddling into warped rooms all wrong.
Who will forgive her for what you did?

Fish Speaking Veneto Dialect

Gastronomists remark that the fish of the Adriatic is amongst the best in the world. And what does the fish have to say about this? Nothing, otherwise what kind of fish is he? As mute as a fish, as the Italian saying goes. We should learn our lesson from this and perhaps not keep silent but chatter a bit less. In the beginning... there was the fish when, just after the year 1000, the Veneto people of the mainland sought refuge on a small group of islands scattered just above the surface of the water around a deep canal, the rivus prealtus. Fish, lots and lots of fish, in Venice and Chioggia, on Murano and Burano, where the humblest fishermen are just like the makers of the most intricate, delicate lace. The fish is a real democrat, his metamorphosis rather adaption to the environment and to the situation. Poor with the poor and rich with the rich. In the past certainly, but today ...it depends, all the world is changing. A history of people seen through fish has not been written yet. But it must include Doge Andrea Gritti (whose massive bulk was painted several times by Titian) who died on 28 December 1538 at the venerable old age of 83, having just eaten an enormous meal of eel on the spit. Pace all'anima sua.

PATINAGE AU POLYGONE – GRENOBLE 1900

They skate because their city is wedged-in
by mountains so grand the winter sunset woos
away all calm. Crenelated orange-pink edges
rip open the sky with spectacular bruises
that heal slowly through the night's consoling hoar.
In long skirts or frock coats, boaters with streamers or
bowlers, tense-backed, they go. How tentative their sport.
They lean right, or left, or out over their toes, quaky,
investigating balance, considering speed.
How hard it is to move at all. Take my hand. Take me.

GET UP, STAND UP

for Robert Nesta Marley

If I cried out would he hear me now among the angelic orders?

If my heart had beaten near his I would have shrunk with dread.

Yet time has brought me this close dizzying nausea,
this obsession of loss, ache for what never was, this, well, love.

Once, all I knew were the songs of struggle, the ones
that sang justice and rights, ones we danced to over and over
all night sweating, stomping in dorms and Cambridge frame houses.

Then, I had no use for love. The world was all prison,
his music all prison break. Only later I came to sway my hips,
to learn the legacy of eros, to want that lover, that face, mutable
diamond — now soft, now fierce — the mulatto face of the first man
I loved. Gone. Both gone now. This mourning unreal and acute.

Now. Now. Now, this is what I imagine. The pot is on the fire.
The bubbles simmer up, simmer down through the stew.
Alive, he might walk in the door, his eyes might open,
I might think, I'll stir it up, I can feed him, let me feed him.
This is what I live for, to feed someone. One man
I fed for years. Small and tight, born in the same season,
he brought me this music, showed me the rebellion. He lives his little
life still. Not too old. And the angel, ancient, has passed.

This is the legacy that lives: If you believe that the Lord
hears what I am saying now, that the children who grew in my belly
and the lights in their eyes come from a larger majesty

then tell me there are no prophets still on earth
that music doesn't tell us what it must be like in Eden.
Past his hard poverty, fighting, I found I could touch my own desire.
Then, past lust, I found the path of music as it takes us to the goodly
tents of the lord and his children. Like dust, like pollen
to me the details of his preaching — a small Ethiopian man king
of kings, the sacraments of kaya, uncombed locks raining from his head.
Though that lion of Judah was yes magnificent, though what we eat
        yes reminds
always of the word, all these are merely the trees that line the road
coming to the righteous strict love of Gd, the highest, the last gift.

Or next to last because in this life you can't forget the past.
Is everything going to be all right because you keep on moving?
Was he Joseph, or Moses, or psalmist David? Perhaps an angel
in some terrible order. Oh, he was a man with no greater
protection than any of us and that is the mystery of the Lord's
punishments. Why begrudge the cars, the women, the
        machete business deals?
I can't. All that doesn't breathe now and he is dead, a foolish
human voice, past all that music that brings the enemy
of our bodies to our souls to demand a more perfect world.
Oh my Gd, I'm older now than he ever was, *than you ever became.*
Hearing a tape of Redemption Song from the last night you sang
for the likes of me, your death comes to me more real ten years out
than ever before and the mourning goes on and on on endless nights.
What I want to ask you is what were you thinking how could you let it go
like that, the cancerous toe
the whole body eaten, no you may be redeemed, we may sing
we'll be forever loving Jah, but you are gone
for us to accept what we can never understand.
And that miraculous music, the miraculous preaching that leads me
to the simple, the grand, the humble "thank you lord for what
you're doing right now." I mean to thank you now. Right now.

WORLD WITHOUT END

If you believe the various records and registers,
on the very morning that the Genoese, in the commission
of King Ferdinand and Queen Isabella of Castile, set
foot on the island of Guanahani-San Salvador-Watling,
Piero della Francesca died at the Via Aggiunti,
in the town of his birth, Borgo Sansepolcro.
If you believe Vasari he was blind. The works
lead us to believe that this Euclidean scholar's
round-bellied women turned finally,
in the "Madonna of the Birth,"
into a sort of Riemannian proposition of beauty.
That enormous-bellied woman in Monterchi
may have been homage to Piero's own mother,
called Francesca or Romana, depending
on whom you believe. And she may have been
buried in the adjoining graveyard the year before
Piero drew the curtains open, held by his familiars,
his constant angels draped in red and green
with alternating, matching socks and wings.
They present one more enigma of Piero —
this utterly peculiar image, a single maternal face
of fear, peace, desperation, patience, exhaustion.
Beneath the bursting drapery of her blue dress,
a slit of white underdress covers a belly
expectant, low and round like the globe.
I believe the third Book of the Dead
of the Confraternity of San Benedetto,
which registers the end on 12 October 1492, and
I believe he left this world in peace at the very moment
Columbus was confounded by the roundness of the earth.

And so believe that the master of perspective
closed his part of the Renaissance, a birth
in the Old World and a life that so loved
the even older East of Constantinople,
by ceding spirit to the new one, mother
of all manner of strange round fruit,
its baskets of tomatoes, corn kernels, potatoes,
and to what was being born there, a new form of innocence,
three dimensions of roundness where everything converges
without parallel lines. And where the son of my
future was, remains, and becomes a mystery of flesh.

A FEW YEARS BEFORE THE END

It lifted the way steam rises
from custard, from the mixture
on the stove, the way the milk and eggs
after so much heat and stirring finally
give up, sigh, release one concentrated
bit of energy. So her depression
lifted as if she breathed and saw
something beautiful, the cheerful flirtatious
woman she was, the young woman entertaining
Russian soldiers who couldn't believe
she was a Jew. She didn't believe
she was back in Zloczow in 1914, no,
it was 1989 while she laughed at
the silent hospital tv — "I don't understand
what they are saying, but
they are very funny." That February, every day
was New Year's Eve and my grandmother wanted
to know what I was wearing. "Me,"
she said, "I'm too old to go out."
But it wasn't so simple the way it
lifted. She'd had an overdose
of aspirin trying
to stop a constant headache.
Too much salt transformed the glazed
woman who would clutch the hand of her first
greatgrandson, weeping no words, and it was lovely
to have her back, partly, the fingers
moving, never letting things go.
She was happy, interested, out of it.

Every night I'd come back from the hospital
and rock that infant in my arms.
He'd look up at me with solemn eyes, the stubborn
refusal to sleep, to relinquish his hold
on the world he'd just entered.
And every night I'd shake him down, take
him away from us, take away from him
this thing, this difficult place
he'd cried in for three months straight
till finally his muscles relaxed,
he pulled away, he pulled in,
he gave up, he let go his breath
rising from him like custard steam.

LET ME IN

What goes on inside those ambulance boxes,
those little worlds of activity negotiating the traffic?
I've always been awkward about pulling to the side,
wedging myself between a pillar of the El
and a van, or too slow to take the shoulder.
For three minutes the ambulance wailed
my grandmother to the hospital less than three blocks away
but across and around the parkway.
"Oy vey," she gasped, fell back
on her bed and became so light my mother
could move her. The year before when she'd fallen
on the way to the bathroom and broken
her ribs, she was impossible to move,
her thick legs splayed, the ulcerous flesh,
the heavy breasts still alive.
But oh vey, and that was it, except
for a technicality machines sustained.
That day my period had come, I was trying
to conceive, and the failure became dating
of the pregnancy I did have.
It wasn't a girl I could name for her
but somehow he was she, somehow, she still there.
The laugh, this boy's clear blue eyes —
they're hers. At least I can believe so.
The ambulance couldn't do anything for her.
Still they go past now, in every one a little story,
a little store window of pain,
there they go, taking someone, no her, her, her.
I pull over, I want to follow them this time,
this time it's she. That's where she's gone, it's she. Let me in.

ONLY IN NEW YORK

Can't anyone do something about this
I demanded to the room, to the Asian attending physician
Dr. Jew, to the nurse who could hardly bother
holding the pan to catch my acid vomiting,
to my husband. The LCD readout of the monitor
informed me my contractions
were strong and nearly endless.
So I closed my eyes, shaking and shivering.
No one could do anything and it was getting worse and worse.
I trembled and held hands. Just two hours
in the hospital and he came out. Really too late
they gave me an epidural. Mt. Sinai is so good
at them, both times someone in training
took slow instructions as I held still, pain throwing my body,
the student asking "like this?" as I imagined what would
become of me if I jerk when the needle
goes in my spine. Can't anyone do something about this?
All of life in New York, the lousy subways, the petty
stealing, the terrible stealing, all the terrible ways people
get hurt, lose their lives. Can't anyone do anything about this?
We complain. I've counted twenty Op-ed pieces
on car problems, cars stolen, broken into, towed, ticketed.
The crooked banks, the closed libraries,
the rat-infested parks. Even for us lucky ones, everything
a mess, we demand change of the pain
in our lives. We don't expect to get it. So having a baby,
my choice, becomes part of the general life
of New York. What a pain, what a pain.

LULLABY AFTER NURSING

At first like a late-medieval saint.
Oh my brand new cleric, oh my darling bishop.
But sculpture from the treasury, small, quaint.
Oh my sweetest relic, oh my rarest gift.

Chin tucked in neck, eyelids smooth as beans.
Well satisfied. Your resting hands, one cupped
in the other as, when a four-month fetus, you brought
them to the waves of the ultrasound machine.

And now you sleep so otherworldly deep.
Oh my softest dew, oh my murmuring stream.
Your smile rising up, flickering in dream.
Oh my lovely lamb, oh my own dear Sam.

HOT

One moment it was hot. Hot. Hot.
It was the only adjective you'd gotten
down, heavy, aspirated, breathy aitch
and everything you saw or touched or tasted
was hot. The word to describe all properties
of all things, nature, feeling, your feeling.
A sign. Emotion. Your emotion, caught
in the knot of this word, this listen-to-me. Hot.
But later, instead of murmuring patter
as you toddled, the words began to matter.
One night in a fit of desperation as you
tried to keep us with you in your room,
standing in the crib long after supper,
you discovered talking. Horse. Your eyes lit up,
a brilliant ploy. Yes, horse, now sleep.
Car. Now pointing to the cars on your sheets.
Balloon. And Dog. Looking, pointing, engaging.
Ah, yes, we sigh, if *we* could only act your age.

WHY

You started asking, much too young, this "why."
We all dismissed the possibility
you knew what our sober answers meant.
(You barely had a single sentence down.)
"Why" was merely discourse — the frame
of how one spoke, the way we might behave
the way that "please" can mean "I want." So here
this "why" became a stubborn independence.
It also means "I want" and your cooing "oh"
in answer to some curt "because:" ("it's dirty"
or "here it's dangerous") seemed clear form
and murky substance. You won't remember then
the day you shocked me. With a baby crying
near you in the store you turned and said
that word. You won't remember how belief
was forced on me. You didn't know. How could
you then since all that you'd asserted with
your first word, "me," was so misunderstood.
Here too your "why" the later token of
your eerie hard inquiring selfish mind.

CLEANING SABBATH POULTRY

Is the betrayal the familiar one —
that what I watched with daily scorn I have
become? That now my fingers clean
my chickens, pluck and gut them with the same
fierce casual fury of work that must be done?
Was it her sigh "oh some day you will do
it too" to answer my disgust at her
life as she saw it?
                    The things I've grown
to do. I couldn't imagine what she said
to her mother every day though mostly then
I heard the phone calls as a dim low drone
and when I listened close the empty words
were words for word's sake. Still today I can't
imagine what it is I say to her
in our daily phone reports. I can't
decide what is exchanged between the words.
Her short vacation leaves me here, bereft
of talk accounting for the children's lives —
there's no one else on earth so clearly fixed
to what they do. The real betrayal isn't
the ephemerally false adult I've grown
to believe myself. It's watching myself unmasked.

"IMAGINARY VIEW"

The mother's eye returned to it over and over: a family
on an outing leans over the rim of Liberty's
torch. Far out white wakes of the little boats
make friendly commas around city life. And beyond,
the span of the great bridge promises everything American
and new. So hung the lithograph's neat, clear, impossible
view. She began to know why
the artist had drawn it that way.
For her, it had been months
of infection and months of antibiotics, drawing
the pink liquid up into the syringe and slowly
extruding it on the tip of a spoon. The very little boy
obediently drawing the pool into his mouth, licking
all the spoon, wiping his lip. His sickroom high over
the city filled with tidbits left
for him. Chalk and chalkboard beside
the bed. He used green chalk, a green of hospitals
and old elementary schools. The books and animals
and songs meant nothing, nor the tokens
— here is the enamel butterfly ring
I carried from our time in China — his great-
grandmother had offered — Take it, it will fit your thumb — .
Then his father brought a tool box to fix the bed and table
and the very little boy passed his fingers
over the washers, the wrenches, the phillips heads,
the finishing nails. A wooden handle, lathed
for the curve of a small hand, had a congenial grip,
and so with the long look of the sick, who know

how to pull themselves into small circles,
who can bore deep into the place around them,
who can nail impulse to tedium
the very little boy asked, "can this be my awl?"

CENTRAL PARK

That look, the child
fixing a long steady gaze on mother,
I've seen it so often,
in stores, in living rooms,
in the most crowded rush-hour subway
as the six-month-old leans back
in the umbrella stroller and out
of the mass of sweaty hovering faces,
locks into the mother with that look
that moves the sun and the other stars.
Frederick Law Olmsted thought the urban
mother and child needed
more than whatever paradise they made
themselves, that in summer they were specially
liable to fall into dangerous disorders
of the bowels, and so built
this Dairy, where my friend
sits nursing her six-month-old girl,
and I offer orange sections to my wild
year-and-half son. And though once this place
would dispense clear wholesome milk,
dysentery free, five cents a glass, and ten
for a bowl of bread and milk, from cows kept
in a nearby stable, the private accommodations for
mothers and children have become public
information center, and we sit on the restored
gothic revival porch.
In a formerly male college
in a predominantly male discipline
we were once freshmen together.

Children really, though we'd have denied it then,
when neither could have predicted
or wanted it for each other or ourself.
The night we sat building models of organic
chemicals, so that we might see how reactions
happen, snapping on the carbons, the huge bromines,
we rehearsed making something in the wild world.
But now I have come to find there *is* no wilderness
in me, a woman who ties down whatever
might be to this wild strange easy limitless
love that took me by surprise. And companionably
side by side it seems we both have carved
within, from the chaos of streets,
from among the pigs and goats of squatters,
from the garbage dumps and bone-boiling works,
a landscaped greensward, bigger than anything
we ever made, have imported plants and trees,
followed the whimsy of glacial outcroppings,
of hills, rambles, follies,
and this we open to our children, to ourselves,
that the wilderness we keep is the one we made.

JUPITER EVENING STAR

They weren't there anymore, the high clouds
we watched out our window at dusk.
From the airport in the distance the planes came
into view, starting as thin needles in air
then flaming out over the bright egg moon
and the flat still-blue sky. The city lay before us
under a blackberry sunset. You're my mother
he said suddenly. Who the cap fits, let her
toss it, I thought in my little girl voice.
And then the brightest thing in the sky rose.

STITCH IN TIME

The needle dropped onto the floor.
Bounced. Its tinny voice came back
through memory as I looked for it,
my eye sifting light and shadow.
Beyond, the voice of the drupel,
the voice of the mother.
And another needle dropped to vinyl,
scratched round and round in the
persistent warmth of the reliquary disc.

5:33

The alert astonished attention to formal feeling
tracked, traced the disposition of ninety-three counts
even as handcuffs were secured over crisp
shirtcuffs poking from the tweed jacket of ivy
league fantasy, of ivory tower life

that he did so well to... that he mimicked
so well... that he so well understood in all its technical
requirements he exploded

and then could mimic the gestures
of a different degreed profession.

###

The sincere, plain single voice
with which they spoke — the mothers,
the sisters, the damaged themselves,
crowded that evening in front of the courthouse
asking that the instruments of personal destruction,
the tools and trickery of firearms, be banned
became a noble note of survival.

The next day, one victim speaking quietly
to the newspaper wondered what it would be like to stand
above him on that train out of Penn
and at Merillon take exact
revenge. And backing away
from that enactment as a memory
ricochetting back to his own blood,

and backing away from all
other electrical, injected permutations
became the even nobler note of survival.

###

To have decided after weeks in the box
he didn't see race —
or live his delusion as a black man —
is to give life to other, banal delusions.
So they didn't see him turning
against that which they won't see
in themselves.

###

He was right as often as he was disastrously,
monstrously wrong in his crystallized
assessments of campus mood, or subway etiquette,
in splitting the "I" from the "he," in paring
the dark heart from the defendant,
in assuming that twelve strangers could see his way,
in dressing as lawyer to hear his own "Mr. Ferguson"
turned, accusatory chin thrust, to "you."

###

When they took him from the train
that December night, in his pockets
was a list and I wasn't on it
though I know people whose names
were, who were perhaps his targets,
the ones he never reached.

And there was the campus joke
that he had simply boarded the wrong
train, or started too soon, or came
over and over to the wrong suit and tie.

A year and a half before that,
I heard his voice on the phone
clear, logical, breathlessly full
of events that had befallen him —
the created wrongs and the real wrongs

and the day after the phone call,
in my stifling June office,
pregnant, I waited for him to come that we
might build one last try to make it right,
to appeal dismissal from the university.

And he never came. Later I learned he
was at the office of a famous activist
lawyer, having given up on white
Jewish faculty advocates in the system.

One day after he never came
I had my second son whose wakeful gaze
would nearly obliterate all memory
of the name, so it would be two days
after the massacre until I remembered.

###

But then, having waited all morning,
big, shifting in my hard chair,
sweat and fury pouring from me,
I picked up the phone, invective forming

in my mouth, and hung up before I had a chance
to chastise and rail, to condescend,
to blame with wounded justice, to threaten

my own life, I suppose, so daily I still wonder why.

LIVE AT RYE PLAYLAND

They were a wedding band, a bad
wedding band. The Satinotes, overweight in
gold lame jackets playing to the crowd
of nostalgia drones. Behind us along
the fairway: the Hall of Mirrors,
Aladino's Magic Carpet, Kiddie Park,
where my children rode fiberglass porpoises
and a little sun-and-moon ferris wheel.
My father had first walked the flowered fairway
fifty years before when this was paradise,
and now he sat urging polite attention to the guitar
riffs. Up and down the aisles
of the out-door theater children
played and an audience came and went. It was hot.
What if, twenty years before, I had been a different
girl and followed my high school graduation
with a trip here — to roll and toss and be scared
in someone's arms. And what if just then Bob Marley,
opening for Bruce Springstein at Max's Kansas City, found
one more gig. And dragged up along the Connecticut River on 95
far from the island of mango and guava and ginger,
those mystical blue skies in benediction over nun-like hills
to play for these people. Too many silly ifs. Very soon
I was to hear Catch A Fire. It didn't matter. I needed
Burnin' before my brain knew fire. And needed many years to ask
how we come to know the fire of others. Or how you make it yourself.
When you close the door it is always you, alone, fighting yourself
and wondering. Do we all wonder? Is this the private sin
against which we turn our heads and weep?

VANDALISM

My sheep was the dragon
and my dragon the sheep.
Neither was happy in the year
he was born.

The detective walked the edge
of parkway, the gold button
on his lapel flaming in the sun,
and nothing was there.

The letters were neat and careful,
though they misspelled "Zionism."
The swastikas were balanced and well shaped.
The glass walls of the children's

classroom were blotted with those red
and black marks
and the sun came mottled through
the paper we'd taped to cover.

The teacher told them
"Someone has *damaged*
the classroom and the synagogue,"
her words slow and tensely neutral.

So graffito should evolve to this.
And we to here — brain
numb, heart racing, waiting
for an oriental or talmudic miracle.

PHILIPS STREET, ANDOVER

Now that the huge old family house is gone, completely gone

and its rooms, and those places we spent ourselves, and you're gone

too, I wonder if you're sad we didn't ever decide to make the
        wreck ours,
scrape the money together, dig in, before we became
        irremediably sour,

before you, in the Spanish cool of your Tampa house,
        fever pocking your brain,
punched fist-sized holes in the wall by the phone, or I,
        in Boston, complained
and threw the phone after a drunken call saying you'd
        missed the last plane up.

That first sight of you, in your mother's new Atlanta house, lent
sharpness to the week-long wedding party for my best friend,
your sister. All day I worked in the kitchen, and slept in a child's bunk
after evenings watching you, explosive and beautiful,
        both of us pretending
indifference as you paced the living room carpet where I
        lay reading in a funk.

Years later, crushed beneath our conflicting temperaments we fled
my Somerville triple decker apartment, to the MFA Eakins show
you, a rough boater in murky water, dismissed those men of long ago.
You were rude and handsome, stubborn and smart. At
        home we fought, went to bed
and emerged later, driving west to the little museum of a
        colonial farmstead

your cousin had restored. Another long nomadic day,
        family history, repose,

long Berkshire walks, and in the wide air I knew with a
        brief sharp dread

you were only one odd piece of a family I loved wholly,
        wholly needed to know.

It was in that Andover house in which I first ate lobster
        and Sunday roast,

saw educated people diligently drowning themselves in martinis
before lunch, it was in that house, that one long night, while crazy
Edith prowled, and in my head prowled your many years of boasting,
that you finally held me, high up in the servant's room
        where you stayed,

at first like a brother, we'd wanted each other so long, as
        the breeze

of night replaced the warm air, its movements like intravenous
sedatives, whispers and hands all night joined familiar house ghosts
and the next morning we fucked one way and then another and
        another for weeks

with the whole gang of summer family around us, noisy
        hosts

among whom we wandered when we wanted the tension
        of separateness. We made

long competitive jogging runs, drenched in sweat or rain,
        explored the debris

the house yielded, returning to that room, that safe center
        of hide and seek.

I have had great houses since. One on the edge of the
        lake where Hannibal

outwitted Gaius Flamminius, where Nonna would kill
        pigeons and begin roasting

them at dawn, caressing the carcasses with a brush made
        of rosemary and tarragon

sprigs. A Cuccagna of perfect apricots, grapes, olives and
        oil, delectable,

and just-laid eggs, red-orange and salty and thick as sex.
                    Another house a mansion

of great ambition and awful tragedies, formal rooms, all
                    the children dead,

the father's head crushed in a railroad accident, the widow's
                    legacy of bad

art helping good. But in the one where Edith walked all
                    night and washed

all day, where we lay down in the children's painting
                    room, your boyhood post,

where we sipped beers in the cool massive working kitchen, tested

the failing grand staircase, I wanted to feel every thing
                    every way I could

and I can't anymore remember the arguments that kept us crossed

against each other in that room, or the acute moments of
                    pleasure that led

me to you over and over, just that I came to you over and
                    over, malleable,

that the dark house became mine as my body became mine
                    when I learned

to meet another in it, that we lost a certain kind of shame,
                    which was the cost

of losing time and coordinates within that house, whose
                    plan was embossed

on my skin. Its personal and public history of so much
                    that New England had bled

into the world kept me moving through the house and
                    the people there,

all of whom I wanted to reach through that attempt we
                    made, ineffable,

to teach me something I almost came to know, knowing
                    nothing, and now have lost.

CUSTARD OF THE PAWPAW

We walked the Chattahoochee, the river
a red mud and the bank a tunnel of steam.
The last bright Sunday rubber rafts
poised like the last pictured rocks the Creek
saw there. The scarlet and white oak, buckeye
and spruce drooped in the heat and we walked
into exhaustion, the inexhaustible fireflies beginning
their cold dance. And we saw
signalling to us the separate rhythms
of their attraction, nearly all
the energy converted to light.

Long ago they filled the darkness
like a host of stars descended
from heaven. No, it was the other
way around, I was in the very midst
of heaven, risen to be with angels.
I was with a different man then.
He wanted me and I didn't him
and it was as if my head had been brought
to the very top of the Lord's tent.

That kind of burden makes you happy and mean.
While we plunged through the murky air
I learned so many punishments for my wants,
for example, simply, feeling them,
or knowing wanting so much
that what we do to avoid filling it
becomes the filling it.
What beautiful cardinals in the cathedral

of that vegetation, you said. How bright
the red ones flew, little evening emblems,
and how quickly the brown ones came to your hand.

But you went on, how I wanted things
the way a man wants them and so would not have power
the way a woman has power. But I have no power
the way a man has power. Oh, what vegetation lived
there, on the banks of that water, the silverbell
and sweetgum, sycamore and chinquapin.
And the pawpaw tree, its fruit always eaten
by scavengers, saying had you been in time,
had you been neither too early or, now, too late,
oh, what a wonderful custard I'd have given you.

AND BOAZ BEGAT OBED, AND OBED BEGAT JESSIE, AND JESSIE BEGAT DAVID

So come to the planting ground, come,
come to the fields of abundance,
the sheaves that I let fall of purpose.
Come that the bright constant grasses of perennial
corn should mix their pikes and tassels,
that a husk should burst with bountiful rows.
Come to the threshing floor, come,
come that the corn which we winnow and eat
be made sweet and productive.
Come that I might spread my skirt over you,
that an August afternoon of cut grasses,
wildflowers, pines and oaks might know clouds
the white of seraphim, generous and wise.
Come to the many greens of the far hills
shifted in rippling shadow and exchange
beneath a sun coupling with those clouds,
that a full moon buffeted in a night
of quicksilver blue should stand
a sentinel of grace and fear.
And to corn that names the fruit of all
edible grasses, the inheritance we redeem,
bring your yellow, still, silent, dawn.

Malleus Maleficarum

As if searching for the detritus
of witchcraft, its tokens,
its suspect hairs, with the violence
of the desperate, they broke up the street
for days whacking away at the pavement
with the primitive sledgehammers
of chain gangs, the hammers of peasants,
each heavy blow on a small piece of concrete,
blow after blow making it crumble under
itself until finally they moved on to the next patch.

We went out and came in each day
to the changing walkways,
while what had been on that pavement,
what the pavement preserved and retained,
was being turned over, reexamined,
the old layer brought down
to dust and an underside of moist earth.

Once a newborn grackle fell
from its nest and lay on the hot
concrete under the sun panting,
its whole two-inch case of flesh
desiccating, the watchworks of its heart,
tremendous beneath the weak breast,
pounding away like mad.

This too composed the spell,
and ripened the uneasy undoing
of the common ground of our needs;
small, darkened, from an old country,
men skilled in the art of their town and family
first destroyed and then poured out
a carpet, fresh impressionable, which came
to dry, porous and brittle, but became
again the unnoticed strength beneath us.

LAZARUS

"That horse was touched by the hand
of Gd. Born strangled by his own
umbilical cord on Christmas Eve
he wasn't breathing, he had no
heartbeat. You can't get deader'n that —
but I left him in the barn and Christmas
morning, damned if that foal wasn't up
on his legs prancing around. I named
him Lazarus. It had to be
Gd that raised that foal.
And then my grandson's pony
broke a leg in a gopher hole.
I went to get my gun but Lazarus
leaned down and kissed the broken leg
and the pony leaped to her feet.
They all come now, farmers with
their chickens, cows, goats and sheep,
their tumors and their tibias.
The star was Big Bertha from
the Daley Circus. Oh she
was their bread and butter and dying
slowly Lord no vet knew
what was killing that elephant. They barely
got to the farm in time and one little quick
kiss — she came back healthy as a horse.
No, they all come and no one can
explain and sure they say it's coincidental
and sure I say He moves in mysterious
ways. That's not the point — it's the
tender eye Lazarus lowers as he nuzzles.
I see it. It's what you do
with what you believe."

EINSTEIN'S CURSE

There is a documentary film where the physicists go up
Mount Washington in lumber jackets to prove relativity
by counting falling mu mesons. They will determine if the rate
of survival from up there to down in the lab is greater
than the Newtonian distance would warrant. Travelling
close to the speed of light, where time seems to last longer
from our point of view, comparatively many particles exist.
And so they *do* measure the properties of relativity!
Grainy and black and white the film is stirring:
The autumn woods. The faithless fact of what we think
we see before us confronting an odd inertia
through other frames of reference. We sat before a fire
in a beautiful mild inn, the unfamiliar drink I ordered
for you balanced on the arm of your chair. All around
us others milled, and their talk became distant air
above us. The air where we were was very close. I was going home
continuously after each next drink. I told the story
of the film changing my life. A lie. I heard your lies,
the credible rustle of cosmic dust, things I'd not heard before.
They were words descending from somewhere. I thought
                    they might
have a brief half-life. That they would disappear.
I thought that the night would erode words like wife and husband
and that we'd be gone past any accounting.
That the first snow would clear on the mountain too.

From the Town of Castle Ruins on the Skirts of the Mountain Range

"Thirty may be about books, my dear,
but forty is about death.
For me it's more than the usual
lungs, liver, heart worn into abuse,
more than the intimate dates with my daughter
like secret love affairs — huddling
towards her lovely face, never knowing
when we'll see each other
again like this, leaning over her, teaching
her a romantic life and hoping her
generation survives what ours leaves.
For me it's the clear signs of debt
that have followed me since I ran out
of the grade school classroom having seen
my cousin's face at the window stare and turn
from me, returning to the house where he removed
his father's revolver and shot himself.
I arrived and the police quarantined the house —
a revolution of increasing silence —
the tremble moving from my knees
to my revolted organs informing me
of what now seems both instinct and duty
driving me to friends who die early,
strokes, heart attacks, all manners of cancer.
How many wills have I executed already,
and how many waking and sleeping dreams
of that simple house I've come so far from
on a muddy road, each step an absurd
habit of sin and hope for redemption.

My aunt and uncle and surviving cousin
left the country, left the implosion
of the place, while the energy
that leapt from the chambers of the gun
through the halls of his body, into the house,
closed in, pushed into me in silence,
and changed me. Like a revolute
leaf appearing on a tree
that remains after years of tacit
exposure to nuclear waste, like the terrible
tree itself still there after everything else goes
and this empty earth revolves cold and dusty."

THE PARK OF THE MONSTERS
(at the gardens of Vicino Orsino
to A. on his unfaithful wife)

It seems you have reached the park
                        of the monsters
and I have come along for instruction
                        in toleration.
We are in Bomarzo. No Beaumarchais,
                        no Beaux Arts
                        no having-a-beau.
There is nothing handsome here.
                        We have entered the overgrown
                        garden of that decadent Count
where an elephant copulates with something much too small.
                        A Giant upturns and rips apart
a ripe eroded girl.
                        The stone fairytale cottage leans hopelessly
                        off center above
the gaping jaw of a whale submerged.
                        So explain your patience
                        I can't understand
as that woman, your wife,
                        goes back and forth between you two.
In this chaotic Eden you want me
                        to learn the way
people give and forgive
                        betrayal,
                        for how she might have opened to
that other man's unknown and unknowing eye glazing
the gift of her body,

a gift of discovery,
                given easily because it doesn't have
to be loved for all it is,
                just caressed,
                        just named, just remarked.
Here you arrive and destroy your luggage
                        since all its provisions stocked
                                by optimism
for years have turned to rubble,
                to the sour taste of coffee
made through yesterday's unwashed pot,
                to a sharp morning sun presenting
two insensible bodies full of sleep
                just so
                        without tenderness, before knowledge
and the day
        wipes them into their usual shapes.
So which pain is greater to live by —
                accepting her terrible freedom,
or the simple dictum of received
                knowledge that
                        marriage is being semper
fidelis like the U.S. Marine Corps
                or a DeBeers diamond.
You tell me that the wholesome-apple embrace of the latter
                        can be lost
                                with one absent-
minded but well-aimed fingernail
                running the circumference of
                        the apple so that the skin
once scored gives way and the fruit
                splits cleanly in two halves.

This is no place for children — not the paltry
                              petting zoo leading to the entrance,
not these awful scenes —
                    so we haven't brought any children with us.
Just us,
        and our own plain songs.
Do you know what you wanted from
                          it once upon a time.
Did you imagine a grim
                living-it-out so you could have
food on the table,
            the game on TV,
                        polished shoes beneath the bed.
Had you lost your nerve being
                    alone, meeting girls being
                            jolly meeting girls.
Did you take a wrong turn knowing
                    the moment you turned
                                the wheel
that this would be a long
                road wrong before you turned
                            around again
and got going where you're going.
                        Did you lean out the window
years and months on this road
                    and see brambles, topiary,
                                broken fountains,
the distorted rocks of a madman's fever carried in the name of
    pleasure
and see how utterly different
                    it was from the flat tidy
road I keep pointing to,
            a road you must have known about,
                            on my map.

I have come here,
        you remind me,
                to learn the subtlety of our intuition
that makes its own rule-lessness in a ruthless
                        place. So I will recognize
                            this lovely shade
is cool but not too cool
            and wonder if the grass would feel nicer
                        on my bare skin.
The surrounding images resolve and I see
                  what the animals are doing.
Their heavy insistence on dirty
            mossy fleshy haunch is a terrible
                  beauty insisting
we must build for ourselves
          always this difficult park,
that we construct the rules
        we live by as we live by
            them, that we do not inherit them whole,
that we do not deduce but remake
        them, massive beaver dams of all
            we think, carrying
from the natural world
      and the world of artifice
      and the world of myth
and the strange chambers
    of our very own bodies,
        from our literal and from our lyrical hearts,
from our livers and from our stomachs,
      from sinew and muscle,
        all the scraps of unwanted,
unmatched, unorderly material
      to compose a still and throbbing world
        of waters dammed.

GRAVES OF LUST

And you came to feed me when I was alone
in the monotony of desert days and I lamented
the way the wandering Jews cried out for flesh
and quails came and the greediest ate and died.

Do you believe in the Lord's revenge? There are many
explanations for faith: trichinosis in pigs, and here,
hemlock the bird loves and tolerates though it will kill
humans if still undigested when the bird is eaten.

Plucked, they have the scrawny nude bodies of Barbie
and Midge, our American princesses, all legs and hair.
How many "mediterranean" girls, handling the plastic,
came to long for that shape, that cool immobility.

Before we understood sex we would throw their hard
bodies on top of each other and twist Barbie and Ken
who seem designed to teach girls that sex involves
a large wardrobe and many changes of clothes.

An Italian cook reported shocking the French chef
of a Hong Kong banquet by her overcooking, the bodies
stuffed with a game dressing of sage and pancetta
and placed in a white wine casserole for over an hour.

The mountain Greeks learned Klephtiko, of thieves,
the quail inside an eggplant together tucked underground
with hot coals so nothing could be seen as evidence
of life, nothing traced, nothing stolen.

For this New Year's meal, a luxury of preparations,
eating late into the night, I searched Arthur Avenue markets
for the real bird, coturnix coturnix, and found the American
one, its call — "Bob White, Bob-Bob White" — its name.

The French hear "Paye tes dettes," pay your debts
as the quail flees danger by running rather than flying
away in the stoical, suicidal gesture of a creature
capable of many gestures and dedicated to monogamy.

Physician Antoine Mizauld, touched by the conjugal
devotion of the birds, recommended that couples extract
the hearts of a pair of quails and wear them
on their bodies as a prescription to get along well.

They love the water and they love the land and they fly
low over islands with muscles made for short trips.
Island-hopping mediterranean birds descending so often
gave the prelate of Capri his name, Bishop of Quails.

Yet we loath our manna and we long for quails.
And there went forth a wind from the Lord
and brought quails from the sea and let them fall
about the camp two cubits from the face of the earth

and the people rose up all that day
and all that night and all the next day
and gathered the quails. He that gathered the least
gathered ten heaps and they spread them abroad

for themselves. While the flesh was yet between
their teeth ere it was chewed the anger of the Lord
was kindled and the Lord smote the people
with a great plague and the name of that place

was called Kibroth-hattaavah — graves of lust —
because there they buried the people that lusted.
And the ones who remained, the ones who knew the promised
land, just stood imagining tenderness in their mouths.

Judith Baumel, the author of one previous book of poems, *The Weight of Numbers*, which won the 1987 Walt Whitman Award of the Academy of American Poets, teaches at Adelphi University and lives in The Bronx.